COOKING *for* TWO

COOKING *for* TWO

Perfect Meals for Pairs

By Jessica Strand

Photographs by Caren Alpert

CHRONICLE BOOKS

Library of Congress Cataloging-in-Publication Data available.

ISBN 978-0-8118-6348-3

Manufactured in China.

Designed by Suzanne LaGasa
Prop styling by Leigh Noe
Food styling by Kevin Crafts
Typesetting by Janis Reed

10 9 8 7 6 5 4 3 2 1

Chronicle Books LLC
680 Second Street
San Francisco, California 94107

www.chroniclebooks.com

TABLE *of* CONTENTS

INTRODUCTION

There's something very special about a quiet, intimate dinner with another person, whether it be your spouse, a date, or a friend. Unlike at a gathering, where you engage with a number of people in many levels of conversation and not everything you serve is specific to each person's palate, when you're with just one person both the level of connection and specificity of taste come fully into play. Suddenly, you're really talking, and there's no way to escape into another conversation. The intimacy you experience is singular, and the meal is often what shapes this time together.

Preparing dishes for two is never as easy as one would imagine. First of all, you're always wondering about amounts. I often use only half, a quarter, or an eighth of a recipe in order not to eat leftovers for the rest of the week—leftovers are terrific, but not for an entire week. I also tend to resort to old standards rather than being inventive, and this happens mostly because of not knowing what would work well in smaller portions. Some recipes simply look too elaborate, take too much time, or require expending too much energy for just two people. Instead of relishing the opportunity to cook without pressure, I make the same chicken piccata or roasted asparagus with a poached egg on top rather than using the time to be creative in the kitchen.

This book comes in handy for two types of cooking. First, it is a recipe guide to use while preparing dinner for a friend, spouse, or date. Once you figure out what you're making, cooking for yourself and one other person can be relatively stress free; just remember to give yourself enough time and to relax. The second way this book can be helpful (and I've included a few tips on page 11) is to show you how to prepare a meal *with* a friend, partner, or spouse in an easy, comfortable way, since cooking on your own is very different from cooking with someone else.

Some couples are seamless in the kitchen: They move with grace and finesse, each finishing his or her own tasks without ever stepping on the other's toes. However, other couples may have the opposite experience, where they want to kill each other by the end of cooking; all they do is argue about the process, and when the meal is complete, they're not even interested in eating.

So how do you create a balance in the kitchen when you're cooking with someone? First, make sure that you both love what you're preparing, so that you are equally excited about eating the finished product. Second, divide up the tasks, allowing each other to do the jobs that each of you feel most comfortable doing. Third, compromise, compromise, compromise—forget trying to keep an exact time frame, or complaining that the onions aren't thin enough, or that the oven should be turned on 10 minutes earlier, or that cheese should be grated right before serving . . . none of these things are going to spoil the taste of the meal, so relax.

I've divided the book into four sections: Simple, Fast, Easy Suppers; One-Pot Dinners; Romantic Meals; and Duo Desserts. Each section takes care of a mood, whether it's a quick last-minute meal like chunky chicken potpie or a rich bowl of spaghetti Carbonara; the simplicity of a pot of turkey black bean chili or a bowl filled with soft succulent lamb shanks; or that special evening where you make a perfect petite rack of lamb with nutty Beluga lentils. And of course, what would any book be without a section devoted just to desserts, in this case for two: think individual, mixed berry shortcakes topped with homemade crème fraîche whipped cream or an airy chocolate and candied ginger soufflé.

To me, sharing a meal is one of life's great pleasures, and to be able to engage in deep conversation and relish a moment amidst the chaos of life is bliss. So for those times when it's "Cooking for Two," let this book be your guide, and enjoy!

Eight Tips for Cooking Together

1. Make the decision together on what you plan to cook.

2. Split up the jobs for preparation; for example, one person can prep the vegetables while the other prepares the fish.

3. Be patient.

4. Give each other enough space to do your jobs.

5. Music is always fun to cook to—again, choose it together.

6. Don't talk on the phone if you're in the middle of cooking. It can easily annoy the other person, or cause you to make a mistake.

7. Set the table. Make whatever you're preparing a special occasion.

8. Relax and enjoy yourselves.

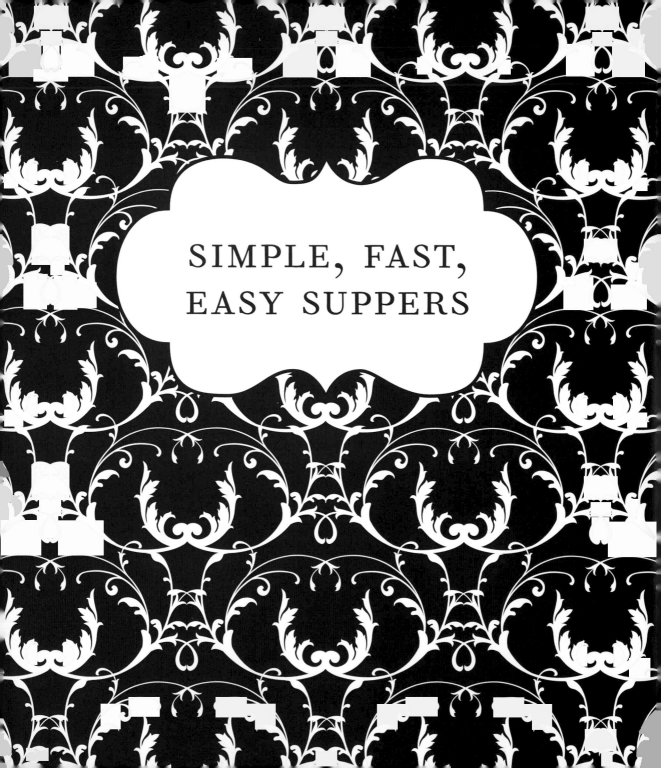

SIMPLE, FAST, EASY SUPPERS

SUGGESTED DRINKS

Pinot Noir (from Oregon or California), Amber beer (try an artisanal variety), crisp white wine like Sauvignon Blanc (from New Zealand or South Africa), or nonalcoholic Cranberry Sour (¼ cup cranberry juice, juice of 1 lime, ice, ¾ cup seltzer or sparkling water)

Antipasti Dinner

My husband and I make a weekly habit of a "nibble night." Either we go out to one of our favorite restaurants and sit at the bar and order appetizers and a glass of wine, or we make our own antipasti platter and dive in when our son goes to bed. Here's one of our favorite spreads.

4 slices sopressata

4 slices prosciutto di Parma

4 slices bresaola

½ cup green olives

½ cup oil-cured black olives

½ cup roasted and salted almonds

4 ounces Parmigiano-Reggiano, cut into chunks

4 ounces Brie

½ baguette, sliced diagonally and toasted

6 piquillo peppers

1 small goat cheese round, about 3 ounces

1 medium fennel bulb, trimmed, halved, cored, and coarsely chopped

½ cup cherry tomatoes, halved

1 tablespoon extra-virgin olive oil

1 teaspoon balsamic vinegar

Salt and freshly ground pepper

On a large decorative platter, arrange the various meats. Place the olives toward the center of the platter, the almonds next to them, then the Parmigiano chunks. Place the Brie on the other side of the platter with a butter knife beside it. Place the bread in a small basket fitted with a napkin to keep warm.

Fill each piquillo pepper with ½ teaspoon of goat cheese, then place the peppers next to the Parmigiano on the platter.

Combine the fennel and cherry tomatoes in a small bowl and drizzle with the olive oil and balsamic vinegar. Sprinkle with salt and pepper, then toss until coated. Place the fennel-tomato mixture next to the piquillo peppers.

Bring a tiny bowl or plate to the table for the olive pits, and serve.

Sweet Potato Cakes with Cherry Tomato, Arugula, and Red Onion Salad with a Tangy Balsamic Dressing

Here's a contemporary version of classic potato pancakes with a sweet, peppery, tangy twist. This is a wonderful choice for brunch, lunch, or dinner.

SWEET POTATO CAKES

1 large sweet potato, peeled and grated on the large holes of a box grater

½ garlic clove, minced

½ teaspoon salt

¼ cup cornstarch, sifted

2 large egg whites

SALAD

½ garlic clove, minced

½ teaspoon Dijon mustard

1 teaspoon grated and finely chopped fresh orange zest

2 teaspoons balsamic vinegar

2½ tablespoons extra-virgin olive oil

Salt and pepper

4 cups arugula

1 cup mixed red and yellow cherry tomatoes, halved

10 paper-thin slices red onion, halved

Canola oil for frying

2 tablespoons sour cream for garnish

FOR THE SWEET POTATO CAKES: In a medium bowl, combine the sweet potato, garlic, and salt, then add the cornstarch.

Using a standing mixer or hand mixer, whip the egg whites on high speed with a tablespoon of warm water until soft peaks form, about 2 to 3 minutes. Fold the egg whites into the potato batter.

FOR THE SALAD: In a medium bowl, combine the garlic, Dijon, orange zest, balsamic vinegar, olive oil, and salt and pepper to taste. Whisk the dressing until emulsified. Add the arugula, cherry tomatoes, and red onion. Toss the vegetables until they are coated.

Fill a heavy pot or deep fryer halfway with oil. Heat the oil to 350°F. If you don't have a thermometer, test the oil by dropping a pea-size bit of batter into it; it should sizzle and crisp, but not burn. If it turns black or dark brown immediately, it is too hot. (Another rule is that if the oil begins to smoke, it's also too hot.)

Place a cooling rack on the counter next to the stove or deep fryer, and arrange a layer of paper towels beneath the rack.

Drop large tablespoons of the batter into the oil; to avoid crowding, fry only about 3 fritters at a time. Fry until golden and crispy, about 3 to 5 minutes, turning once or twice while cooking. Place the fritters on the rack when done and cool for 2 to 3 minutes before serving.

To serve, arrange the salad on plates and place several fritters on top, garnished with a dollop of sour cream.

Quesadillas with Sautéed Radicchio, Manchego, Garlic, and Oregano

You'll enjoy this elegant vegetarian take on the classic cheese quesadilla. The tortilla crisps up like a giant cracker in the oven, which is a nice change from the typical soft quesadilla texture. The slightly bitter, earthy taste of the radicchio pairs well with the tangy bite of the Manchego.

2 tablespoons olive oil, plus more for brushing

2 garlic cloves, minced

¼ teaspoon dried oregano

1 medium head radicchio, halved, cored, and shredded

Salt and freshly ground pepper

8 corn tortillas, 5½ inches in diameter

¾ cup grated Manchego cheese

1 cup cherry tomatoes, quartered

4 tablespoons sour cream

Preheat the oven to 350°F.

Heat the olive oil in a large skillet over medium-high heat. Add the garlic and oregano and sauté until fragrant, about 2 minutes. Add the radicchio and sauté until just wilted, about 4 minutes. Season with salt and pepper to taste. Remove from the heat and set aside.

Lightly brush one side of each tortilla with oil. Place 4 tortillas, oil side down, on a large baking sheet. Spread the radicchio mixture evenly among the tortillas and top each evenly with the cheese. Place the remaining 4 tortillas, oil side up, on top and press down lightly. Bake the quesadillas until heated through and golden brown, flipping once halfway through, about 4 minutes per side. Place in the broiler to brown during the last minute, if desired. Cut the quesadillas into wedges, sprinkle with the cherry tomatoes, and top each with a dollop of sour cream.

A Garbage Salad for Two: Chicken, Garbanzo Beans, Beets, Green Beans, Cucumbers, Avocado, Hearts of Palm, Cherry Tomatoes, Walnuts, and Chopped Romaine with a Creamy Herbal Vinaigrette

My friend Lauren's mother, Penny, uses this funny name for a salad full of leftovers, and I couldn't think of anything more appropriate to call it, except perhaps "The Most Delicious Garbage Salad." The ingredients really depend on what you have handy, so feel free to substitute boiled eggs, salami, tuna, leftover salmon, or whatever you have around. The goal is that in the end, the salad is a meal.

½ cup roasted chicken, both dark and white meat, skinned, boned, and torn into pieces

¼ cup whole garbanzo beans, lightly chopped

½ cup canned or fresh beets, coarsely chopped

1 cup fresh green beans, stemmed, steamed, and halved

1 Persian or Japanese cucumber, sliced into paper-thin disks

¾ medium avocado, cubed

½ cup hearts of palm, sliced into ¼-inch disks

10 cherry tomatoes, halved

10 to 12 walnut halves, toasted and coarsely chopped

5 cups romaine lettuce leaves, chopped into thirds

CREAMY HERBAL VINAIGRETTE

½ shallot, minced

1 teaspoon Dijon mustard

⅛ teaspoon honey

¼ cup sour cream

2 teaspoons heavy cream

3 teaspoons tarragon vinegar

1 ½ teaspoons fresh lemon juice

1 teaspoon chopped fresh dill

1 teaspoon chopped fresh basil

1 teaspoon chopped fresh thyme

Dash of Worcestershire sauce

1 teaspoon grated and finely chopped fresh lemon zest

½ cup olive oil

Salt and freshly ground pepper, to taste

Combine all the salad ingredients in a large salad bowl, then combine all the vinaigrette ingredients in a separate bowl and stir until smooth. Season to taste. Drizzle as much dressing as you like over the top of the salad, thoroughly toss so that the ingredients are coated, and serve. Leftover dressing can be kept in the refrigerator for up to one month.

Sake- and Ginger-Poached Black Bass on a Bed of Garlicky Baby Bok Choy

This elegant dish is delicate and light. If baby bok choy is not available, feel free to substitute spinach or asparagus.

20 baby bok choy leaves, or about 3 to 4 heads baby bok choy

3 tablespoons canola oil

1 teaspoon sesame oil

1 clove garlic, minced, plus 2 cloves slivered

1 tablespoon fresh ginger, peeled and minced

2 cups sake

¼ cup white miso paste

¼ cup mirin

Two 8-ounce black bass fillets

1 teaspoon soy sauce

Prepare a medium steamer with water and bring to a boil. Place the bok choy in the steamer and cook for 5 to 7 minutes, or until tender. Remove from the steamer, and set aside.

In a large saucepan, heat 1 tablespoon of the canola and the sesame oil over medium-high heat. Add 1 clove of the garlic and the ginger and sauté for 1 to 2 minutes or until light gold. Slowly add the sake to the pan, then add the miso paste and mirin, and whisk until completely blended. Reduce to a simmer, and place the fish, skin side down, in the sauce. Spoon the sauce over the fish, then cover and cook for 4 minutes. Lift the lid to check for doneness and continue cooking for 2 to 4 minutes or until just cooked through.

While the fish is cooking, heat the remaining 2 tablespoons of canola oil in a medium sauté pan. Add the 2 cloves of slivered garlic, and brown very slightly, then add the bok choy and sauté for 2 minutes. Add the soy sauce and cook for another minute.

Place the bok choy on two festive dinner plates. Gently place the fish on top and serve.

Grilled Garlic Shrimp with Mâche, Avocado, Fennel, and Red Onion Salad

This dish is so festive looking it can be made for a special occasion or as a last-minute, quickie dinner. It's important to remember that the shrimp cooks very quickly, easily becoming chewy and overcooked. But if you stay on top of the process, you'll have succulent shrimp every time.

SHRIMP

6 large cloves garlic, pressed through a garlic press to make 3 tablespoons

2 tablespoons extra-virgin olive oil

Sea salt and freshly ground pepper

10 jumbo shell-on shrimp (about 1 pound), washed

SALAD

6 cups mâche (5 to 6 ounces)

1 avocado, halved, pitted, and cut into ¾-inch cubes

1 medium fennel bulb, outside layer removed, halved, cored, and thinly sliced

¼ large red onion, thinly sliced, then coarsely chopped

2 tablespoons extra-virgin olive oil

1½ teaspoons balsamic vinegar

½ teaspoon fresh lemon juice

FOR THE SHRIMP: In a medium bowl, combine the garlic, olive oil, ¼ teaspoon salt, and pepper to taste. Add the shrimp, toss to coat, and let marinate for 15 minutes or more.

Preheat the grill to medium high.

FOR THE SALAD: In a medium bowl, combine the mâche, avocado, fennel, and red onion. Drizzle with the olive oil, balsamic vinegar, and lemon juice, and sprinkle with salt. Toss and place on two plates.

Thread 5 shrimp onto each of 2 skewers. Brush with the marinade. Grill for 2 to 3 minutes per side, or until just cooked through.

Place the cooked shrimp on top of the salad, and serve.

Chunky Chicken Potpies with Root Vegetables

I have to admit that one of my favorite dinners as a kid was a frozen chicken potpie. My mother was a terrific cook, but when she was going out for the evening she bought chicken potpie and slipped it into the oven for me. Just puncturing the crust and watching the steam rise was a thrill, and it still is! I cheat a little by using frozen puff pastry dough; it works beautifully and also saves time.

½ cup chopped carrots, cut into ½-inch disks

½ cup parsnips, cut into ½-inch disks

1 small Yukon gold potato, peeled and cut into bite-size cubes

1 tablespoon olive oil

Salt and pepper, to taste

2 boneless chicken breasts, or 1 cup cubed leftover cooked chicken

3 tablespoons chicken stock, plus 1 cup

2 tablespoons butter, plus 2 tablespoons, melted, for glazing

¼ cup flour

½ cup half-and-half

1 tablespoon minced yellow onion

½ teaspoon minced fresh thyme

1 tablespoon dry sherry

½ cup frozen petite peas

1 tablespoon coarsely chopped fresh Italian parsley

1 (9-ounce) sheet frozen puff pastry, defrosted according to package directions

Prepare a steamer. When the water comes to a boil, place the carrots, parsnips, and potato in the steamer basket and steam until just tender, about 8 to 10 minutes. Rinse in cold water and set aside.

If using chicken breasts, add the olive oil and salt and pepper to a small skillet and heat over medium-high heat. Place the chicken breasts in the pan and sauté for 3 to 4 minutes, turn over, and add the 3 tablespoons of chicken stock. Cover and let cook for an additional 6 to 8 minutes, or until cooked through. Set aside to cool, then cut into chunks or shred.

Preheat the oven to 400°F.

In a medium saucepan, melt the 2 tablespoons of butter, then slowly add the flour, stirring constantly; do not allow it to brown. Slowly add the half-and-half, the remaining cup of chicken stock, onion, and thyme. Continue stirring while the sauce thickens, about 3 minutes. Then add the sherry and allow to cook off for 1 to 2 minutes.

Add the chicken, root vegetables, peas, and parsley to the sauce and cook for 2 to 3 minutes until all the ingredients are fully blended.

Divide the filling between two ovenproof (12-ounce) bowls. Cut and fold a piece of the puff pastry over the top, securing it to the sides of the bowl by pinching it. Paint the pastry with the butter, then place in the oven.

Bake the pies for 20 to 25 minutes, or until the tops are puffy and golden.

Spaghetti Carbonara with a Poached Egg on Top

My father's favorite dish to prepare is carbonara. He keeps revising his recipe. He must have at least eight versions of the dish to date. Most recently he prepared it with a raw yolk on top. I realize this may scare off a few of you, so as an alternative, I've chosen to poach the egg, which gives the same rich, gooey effect.

½ cup finely grated Parmigiano-Reggiano

2 tablespoons finely grated Pecorino Romano

1 tablespoon coarsely chopped fresh Italian parsley, plus more for garnish

3 ounces guanciale or pancetta (or high-quality bacon if neither are available), cut into ⅓-inch cubes

2 teaspoons olive oil

½ red onion, coarsely chopped

3 tablespoons dry white wine

8 ounces spaghetti

2 tablespoons white or rice vinegar

2 large eggs

Sea salt and coarsely ground black pepper

Place the cheeses and 1 tablespoon parsley in a bowl.

In a heavy skillet over moderate heat, cook the guanciale until the fat begins to render and it begins to become brown and crispy, about 7 to 10 minutes. Pour off half the fat, and add the olive oil. Heat for 1 minute, then add the onion. Stir occasionally until translucent and golden, about 12 to 15 minutes. Add the wine and simmer for 2 minutes. Set aside.

In a large stockpot filled with boiling, salted water, cook the spaghetti until al dente. About 4 minutes before the spaghetti is done, poach the eggs.

To prepare for poaching, add 1½ to 2 inches of water to a large skillet and place over medium heat until the water comes to a light boil, then add the vinegar. Wait for 1 minute, then add the eggs by cracking each into a saucer and carefully slipping the egg into the water. Let the eggs cook for 4 minutes. If the yolks still look too runny for your liking, spoon water on top of the eggs and cook for another 30 seconds. Remove the eggs carefully from the water with a slotted spoon.

Drain the pasta and place it back in the pot. Toss the pasta with the guanciale mixture, and then toss with the cheese mixture. Serve the pasta in two large soup or pasta bowls. Place a poached egg on top of each serving. Salt and pepper each bowl to taste, sprinkle with the remaining parsley, and serve.

Pan-Seared, Herb-Rubbed Pork Chops
with Port-Glazed Apples

On a cold autumn or winter night this supper will warm every inch of you and fill the air with the smell of apples. I like to apply quite a bit of pressure while dredging the pork chops in the herbs so that they end up searing right into the meat.

1 Granny Smith apple, peeled, halved, and cored

2 teaspoons coarsely chopped fresh rosemary leaves

2 teaspoons coarsely chopped fresh thyme leaves

⅛ teaspoon sea salt

⅛ teaspoon freshly ground pepper

Two 1-inch-thick pork rib chops

2 tablespoons butter

Large pinch of sugar

2 tablespoons, plus ½ cup tawny port

½ cup chicken broth

Slice the apple halves from top to bottom into ½-inch-thick slices.

Place the herbs and salt and pepper on a large plate; mix the spices with your hands. Dredge the pork chops in the mixture, pressing the herbs into the meat.

Melt 1 tablespoon of the butter in a large, heavy skillet over medium heat. Stir in the sugar and 2 tablespoons of the port. Let the ingredients meld together for 1 to 2 minutes. Add the apples and let them cook, turning them periodically, until they are golden and soft in texture, about 10 to 12 minutes. Transfer the apples to a plate lined with wax paper so they don't stick.

Add the remaining tablespoon of butter to the skillet over medium heat. Let the butter brown slightly, then add the pork chops. Cook the pork chops for 5 to 6 minutes per side, or until they are browned and firm to the touch but slightly pink inside. Put the pork chops to the side.

Add the ½ cup port and chicken broth to the skillet; turn up the heat so it reduces quickly, letting the sauce simmer. When the sauce has thickened and reduced by half, after about 2 to 3 minutes, add the pork chops and apples back to the skillet. Turn to coat both in the sauce, then place each chop on a plate, spoon the apples and juices over the meat, and serve.

Lamb Chops with Mint Gremolata

To me, a lamb chop is a perfect food. It has all the essentials: complexity of flavor and texture and a satisfying heft that comfortably fills you. This dish goes well with a beet, red onion, fennel, and avocado salad.

Four 1-inch-thick lamb chops, at room temperature

1 garlic clove, cut in half, plus 1 large clove, minced

3 tablespoons olive oil

Sea salt and freshly ground pepper

2 tablespoons finely chopped fresh Italian parsley

2 tablespoons finely chopped fresh mint

1 teaspoon grated and finely chopped fresh lemon zest

2 teaspoons fresh lemon juice

Rub the lamb chops on all surfaces with the garlic halves. Drizzle the lamb with 1 tablespoon olive oil, and then season it with salt and pepper to taste.

In a large skillet, heat 2 tablespoons of the olive oil on medium-high heat until sizzling. Add the lamb chops and cook for 3 minutes per side for rare, 4 minutes per side for medium.

In a small bowl, combine the parsley, mint, lemon zest, and lemon juice, and season with salt and pepper to taste. Stir until blended.

Place the chops on plates, sprinkle with the gremolata, and serve.

The Ultimate Burger with Havarti Cheese, Caramelized Onions, and Sautéed Mushrooms Served with Fennel and Cucumber Slaw

Sinking your teeth into a juicy, cheesy burger overflowing with golden sweet onions and succulent mushrooms—what could be better? The flavors meld in your mouth, creating the "ultimate" burger experience. As for the slaw, I pile it on top of all the garnishes, but you certainly can put it on the side for a cool, crunchy side dish.

BURGERS

¾ pound ground beef
(15 percent fat)

2 teaspoons Worcestershire sauce

⅛ teaspoon salt, plus more to taste

⅛ teaspoon freshly cracked pepper, plus more to taste

2 tablespoons olive oil

½ large yellow onion, thinly sliced into disks

12 button mushrooms, cleaned and thinly sliced

1 teaspoon fresh thyme leaves

SLAW

1 small fennel bulb, trimmed, halved, cored, and cut across in ¼-inch slices

2 Persian cucumbers, sliced into ⅛-inch disks

1 tablespoon grated and finely chopped fresh orange zest

2 tablespoons olive oil

1 teaspoon balsamic vinegar

1 teaspoon fresh orange juice

Salt and pepper

2 English muffins

2 to 3 large slices Havarti cheese

FOR THE BURGERS: In a medium bowl, combine the ground beef, Worcestershire sauce, salt, and pepper. Mix together thoroughly with your hands and form two large burgers. Set aside.

In a large sauté pan, heat the olive oil over medium heat. Add the onions, sauté until they begin to become translucent, about 5 minutes, then add the mushrooms, thyme, and salt and pepper to taste. Cook the mixture until browned, about 10 minutes. Take the pan off the flame.

FOR THE SLAW: In a medium bowl, combine the fennel, cucumbers, and orange zest. Add the olive oil, balsamic vinegar, orange juice, and salt and pepper to taste. Toss the vegetables until coated with the dressing.

Preheat the grill to medium high. At the same time toast the English muffins.

Grill the burgers to desired doneness, about 4 minutes per side for medium-rare. When the burgers are 2 minutes shy of being done, place the cheese on top of the burgers and close the grill top. When you open the grill the cheese should be melted.

To serve, place the English muffin bottoms on plates, followed by the burgers, then the mushrooms and onions and all of the condiments you desire, then place the remaining muffin halves on top. Serve up the fennel and cucumber slaw, and you're ready to eat!

Vegetable Curry with Roasted Almonds, Golden Raisins, and Basmati Rice

This is comfort food with an exotic twist. You certainly can use other vegetables in the curry, such as broccoli, zucchini, or potatoes. The important thing is to think of the textures and how they balance each other out.

2 tablespoons sliced almonds

2 tablespoons golden raisins

4 tablespoons olive oil

1 small onion, cut into small dice

1 heaping teaspoon fresh ginger, finely grated

1 tablespoon curry powder

2 teaspoons sugar

1 cup coconut milk

Sea salt

½ cup basmati rice

2 Japanese eggplants, cut into ¼-inch disks

2 cups chopped cauliflower, cut into small florets

1 cup chopped carrots, cut into ½-inch disks

½ bunch medium-thick asparagus, woody bottoms removed, stems cut into thirds

Preheat the oven to 350°F and arrange a rack on the upper shelf of the oven.

Place the almonds in a pie tin and set in the middle of the upper rack of the oven. Cook the almonds 2 to 3 minutes, or until golden brown. Let cool.

In a small bowl, combine the raisins with boiling water to cover and allow to plump for 20 minutes, then drain, pat dry, and set aside.

In a small sauté pan, heat 2 tablespoons of the olive oil. Add the onion, ginger, curry powder, and sugar and sauté for 1 to 2 minutes. Add the coconut milk and let the sauce simmer over medium-low heat for 10 minutes. Add salt to taste, and set aside.

Cook the basmati rice according to the package directions.

In a large saucepan, heat the remaining 2 tablespoons of olive oil over medium heat until it begins to shimmer. Place the eggplant slices in the pan and let them quickly brown for 3 minutes per side. Add the cauliflower and carrots and sauté for 2 minutes, then add ½ cup water, cover, and cook for an additional 5 minutes, or until the vegetables are tender. Add the asparagus and stir, then cover and cook for 4 to 5 minutes more. Add the coconut sauce to the vegetable mixture, stir, and cook for an additional 2 to 3 minutes. Fold the raisins and almonds (reserving 2 teaspoons of the almonds) into the curry.

Serve the rice in two large pasta bowls, spreading the grains to create a flat surface. Pour the vegetable curry over the rice and garnish each bowl with a teaspoon of toasted almonds.

ONE-POT DINNERS

SUGGESTED DRINKS

Chianti, Sancerre wine, or nonalcoholic Pomegranate Fizz (¼ cup pomegranate juice, ¾ cup sparkling water, and juice of ¼ lime)

Onion Soup with Loads of Thyme and Giant Gruyère Crostini

Whenever the weather begins to get cold, I fantasize about the perfect bowl of French onion soup. The top is golden and crisp, the cheese has blistered and fallen and is completely melted, and gooey bits are stuck to the outer sides of the bowl. When I cut through the cheese, the bread is slightly crisp, but mushy at the same time. I fill my spoon with the rich, full broth crammed with soft, sweet, smoky onions. Here's my fantasy in a bowl.

1 pound yellow onions, halved and thinly cut lengthwise

3 to 5 sprigs fresh thyme

1 bay leaf

¼ teaspoon sea salt

Freshly cracked pepper

1 teaspoon all-purpose flour

½ cup dry white wine

2 cups beef stock

1 cup water

1½-inch-thick slice of ciabatta cut in half

2 tablespoons unsalted butter

1½ cups grated Swiss Gruyère cheese

In a heavy 5-quart pot, melt the butter over low heat. Add the onions, thyme, bay leaf, salt, and pepper to taste and cook, stirring occasionally, until the onions are deep amber in color and exceedingly soft, 25 to 30 minutes. Add the flour and cook for 1 to 2 minutes, then add the wine, increase the heat, and let the wine cook, for 2 to 3 minutes. Add the beef stock and water, and let the soup simmer for 25 to 30 minutes, allowing the flavors to meld together. Season again with salt and pepper to taste.

Preheat the oven to broil. Arrange a rack in the middle of the oven.

Place the ciabatta on the middle rack of the oven and toast until crispy, about 2 to 3 minutes per side.

Remove the bay leaf and thyme sprigs from the soup and discard. Pour the soup into two ovenproof bowls, float the toasted ciabatta on top, and cover it with a thick layer of the Gruyère. Put the soup bowls under the broiler on the middle rack and cook for 3 to 5 minutes, or until the cheese is fully melted and golden.

Creamy Fish Chowder with Fennel
Served with Crispy Garlic Bread

Though I love New England clam chowder and oyster stew, they're a bit too rich for me, so here's my lighter alternative—with as much flavor or maybe even more.

2 slices thick-cut bacon, cut into 2-inch pieces

2 teaspoons olive oil

1 leek, cleaned well, white parts only coarsely chopped

1 carrot, finely chopped

1 medium fennel bulb, trimmed, halved, cored, and diced

24 ounces fish stock or clam juice

¼ to ½ teaspoon saffron threads

¼ cup heavy cream

12 ounces firm white fish such as halibut or cod, boned and skinned, cut into 1-inch cubes

3 tablespoons coarsely chopped fresh Italian parsley

Crispy Garlic Bread (facing page)

In a cast-iron or heavy enamel stockpot or stew pot, cook the bacon over medium heat until crispy, about 5 to 7 minutes. Transfer to paper towels to drain. Drain the bacon fat from the pan. Add the olive oil and heat over medium heat. Add the leek, carrot, and fennel and sauté until the leek is translucent, about 7 to 10 minutes.

Add the fish stock and saffron to the pot. Bring to a simmer and cook for 10 minutes. Add the cream and bacon and let simmer a few more minutes. Add the fish and cook for 10 minutes, or until opaque in the center.

Ladle the chowder into two bowls. Sprinkle with the parsley, and serve with the Crispy Garlic Bread.

Crispy Garlic Bread

1 small French roll

1 tablespoon olive oil

1 medium garlic clove, halved

Pinch of sea salt

Preheat the oven to 400°F and arrange a rack on the upper shelf.

Halve the roll as if you're making a sandwich. Place the bread halves crust side up in the center of the top rack and toast for 3 to 4 minutes. Brush the cut sides of the bread with olive oil. Put back into the oven and toast for another 3 to 4 minutes or until golden.

Rub the garlic clove over both sides of the crispy bread, sprinkle with sea salt, and serve.

Black Bean Turkey Chili with Corn Muffins and Whipped Honey

This rich, aromatic chili warms the body in a flash. I love it paired with crumbly corn muffins spread thickly with honey. The earthy flavors of the chili blend beautifully with the sweet, nutty taste of the corn muffins. This can be made one day ahead and refrigerated, or up to three weeks ahead and frozen.

2 tablespoons olive oil

¾ large yellow onion, coarsely chopped (about 1½ cups)

2 large cloves garlic, minced

½ large yellow bell pepper, chopped

1 teaspoon ground cumin

1 pound ground turkey

½ tablespoon chili powder

½ teaspoon cinnamon

2 (15-ounce) cans black beans, well drained

1 (14½-ounce) can diced tomatoes with their juices

Salt and pepper

OPTIONAL GARNISHES

2 tablespoons sour cream

2 tablespoons grated sharp cheddar cheese

2 tablespoons sliced red onion

Corn Muffins (page 44)

Whipped Honey (page 44)

Heat the oil in a large, heavy pot over medium-high heat. Add the onion, garlic, bell pepper, and cumin. Sauté until the onion is soft and golden, stirring frequently, about 10 minutes. Add the turkey and brown for 10 minutes, then stir in the chili powder and cinnamon. Add the black beans and tomatoes with their juices, and bring to a boil. Reduce the heat to medium. Simmer uncovered until the liquid is reduced by half, stirring occasionally, about 30 minutes.

Transfer 2 cups of the chili to a food processor. Blend to a coarse paste, then return to the pot. Simmer the chili to thicken further, if desired.

Season the chili with salt and pepper to taste. To serve, spoon into two large soup bowls, garnish with the toppings, as desired, and arrange the Corn Muffins alongside.

Corn Muffins

½ cup cornmeal

½ cup unbleached all-purpose flour

⅛ cup sugar

⅛ teaspoon salt

½ tablespoon baking powder

½ cup buttermilk

1 large egg, lightly beaten

2½ tablespoons melted butter, plus 2 teaspoons

Whipped honey to serve

Preheat the oven to 375°F.

Sift the dry ingredients into a medium bowl. Add the buttermilk, egg, and 2½ table-spoons melted butter and stir until the dry ingredients are moistened. Don't overmix the batter.

Use the remaining 2 teaspoons of butter to grease half of the cups in a muffin tin.

Fill six muffin cups halfway with the corn batter.

Bake the muffins until golden and a tooth-pick inserted in the center comes out clean, 15 to 17 minutes. Remove from the oven and let cool in the pan for 5 to 10 minutes. Slice thickly, if desired, and serve warm with whipped honey.

Yields 6 muffins.

Whipped Honey

½ stick unsalted butter

2 tablespoons honey

Soften the butter. Add the honey and fold it into the creamy butter. Keep creaming the two together until completely blended.

Place the mixture in a small dish, level off with a knife, and place in the refrigerator until 15 minutes before serving.

Italian White Bean, Escarole, and Pancetta Soup Smothered in Parmesan Cheese

This recipe makes 4 large servings, enough for leftovers the next day, but if I were you I'd double the recipe and freeze the extras. Add the cheese after you've heated the soup. It's a perfect cozy dinner with a glass of earthy, Italian red wine.

1 tablespoon olive oil

1 medium yellow onion, coarsely chopped

2 cloves garlic, thinly sliced, plus 1 large clove, pressed through a garlic press

Two ½-inch-thick slices Italian pancetta, coarsely chopped

2 carrots, sliced diagonally ⅛ inch thick

2 parsnips, sliced diagonally ⅛ inch thick (if large, halve them)

1 large head escarole (1 pound), tough ribs discarded and leaves thinly sliced

4 cups chicken or vegetable stock

1 cup water

1 (16-ounce) can Italian white beans (cannellini), rinsed and drained

1 teaspoon dried rosemary

Sea salt and freshly ground pepper

1 cup freshly grated Parmesan cheese

Warm the olive oil in a medium stockpot over medium-low heat, then add the onion and sliced garlic and sauté until translucent, about 4 to 5 minutes. Add the pancetta and let crisp, about 8 to 10 minutes. Add the carrot and parsnip slices, and stir the mixture for 1 minute. Add the escarole and sauté for about 2 minutes or until wilted. Add the stock and water and bring to a boil, then add the white beans and rosemary, and simmer uncovered for about 15 to 20 minutes. Take half the soup and place it in a blender. Blend until smooth, then return to the pot. Stir in ½ cup of the Parmesan cheese, the pressed garlic, salt and pepper to taste.

Ladle the soup into two large soup bowls. Sprinkle the top of the bowls with the remaining Parmesan cheese, and serve.

Gratin of Eggplant Layered with **Plum Tomatoes, Fresh Mozzarella,** and **Lemon-Basil Pesto**

You don't need to be a vegetarian to crave this gratin for dinner. I like to serve it with a crisp escarole salad. Use an 8-by-8-inch baking dish, or if you've got a small gratin dish, that will work beautifully as well.

2 tablespoons pine nuts

2 cloves garlic, coarsely chopped

½ cup freshly grated Parmesan cheese

1 cup coarsely chopped fresh basil

1 teaspoon fresh lemon juice

Salt and freshly ground pepper

1 large eggplant, sliced lengthwise into eight ¼-inch-thick slices

2 tablespoons olive oil, plus 1 teaspoon

10 plum tomatoes, sliced ¼ inch thick

2 balls (about 12 ounces) fresh mozzarella, thinly sliced

Preheat the oven to 375°F. Arrange a rack on the upper shelf of the oven.

Spread the pine nuts on a pie tin and place on a rack set on the upper shelf of the oven. Watching carefully, toast for 3 to 4 minutes, or until golden brown. Set aside and allow to cool before processing.

In a blender or food processor, purée the pine nuts, garlic, Parmesan cheese, basil, and lemon juice until fully combined. Season with salt and pepper to taste. Set aside.

Lightly salt the eggplant slices and place them on a bed of paper towels for 30 minutes to let the salt leach the bitterness from the eggplant. Rinse and pat dry.

Heat the 2 tablespoons olive oil in a large sauté pan over medium heat. Adding 2 to 3 eggplant slices at a time so they can brown evenly, brown on both sides, 3 to 4 minutes per side. Place on fresh paper towels to drain.

Lightly grease a 2-quart baking or gratin dish with the remaining teaspoon of olive oil. Arrange half of the eggplant in the bottom, top with half of the tomato slices, then spread with half of the lemon pesto, and top with half of the mozzarella slices. Repeat.

Place the dish in the oven and bake for 30 to 35 minutes, or until golden and bubbling.

Lasagna for Two with Spinach, Ricotta, and Wild Mushrooms

This lasagna sounds complicated, but even though it has a lot of stages, it's incredibly simple. I like to make separate layers of mushrooms, ricotta, and spinach, but feel free to mix it up. This can be made two days ahead and refrigerated, or up to a month ahead and frozen.

1 (16-ounce) package frozen chopped spinach

7 ounces ricotta cheese

1 cup (about 2½ ounces) freshly grated Parmesan cheese

1 large egg

½ teaspoon salt

Freshly ground pepper

¼ teaspoon nutmeg

3 tablespoons olive oil

10 to 12 shiitake mushrooms, cleaned and sliced

8 to 10 cremini mushrooms, cleaned and sliced

8 to 10 oyster mushrooms, cleaned and sliced

8 to 10 fresh button mushrooms, cleaned and sliced

2 tablespoons chopped fresh Italian parsley

1 tablespoon chopped fresh thyme

1 pound fresh plain lasagna sheets

1½ to 2 cups Quick Tomato Sauce (recipe follows)

1½ cups shredded fresh mozzarella

Preheat the oven to 375°F.

Place the frozen spinach in a saucepan with 2 tablespoons water and heat over medium-low heat. Bring to a simmer, cover, and cook for 2 minutes. Push down the spinach, breaking up any frozen chunks, and add a tablespoon or two of water if needed. Cover the pan again, and cook until completely defrosted, about 3 more minutes.

Put the spinach in a large colander and squeeze the water out with the back of a large metal or wooden spoon. When the spinach is dry in texture (not mushy), place in a large bowl. Stir in the ricotta, ¾ cup of the Parmesan, and the egg, and season the mixture with ¼ teaspoon of salt, pepper to taste, and the nutmeg. Set aside.

Warm the olive oil and the remaining ¼ teaspoon of salt in a large saucepan over medium heat for 1 minute, then add all of the mushrooms. Sauté the mushrooms for about 15 minutes, or until they have expelled their juices and become golden. Add the parsley and thyme and cook for another 2 minutes. Set aside.

If your fresh pasta is in the form of large sheets, cut them into strips to fit the size of your glass dish so that you will have enough noodles for four layers of lasagna.

Fill a stockpot halfway with water and bring to a boil. Cook 4 lasagna noodles at a time, following the package directions for doneness.

On the bottom of a 2-quart (8-inch) glass baking dish, spread a layer of tomato sauce (about ½ cup), followed by enough noodles to cover, then half of the spinach mixture. Add another layer of noodles, ½ cup tomato sauce, and all of the mushroom mixture. Add a third layer of noodles, ½ cup tomato sauce, and the remaining spinach mixture. Top with a final layer of noodles, the remaining tomato sauce, the mozzarella, and the remaining ¼ cup Parmesan.

Line a baking sheet with aluminum foil and place the lasagna on top. Bake for 25 to 30 minutes, or until golden and bubbling.

Quick Tomato Sauce

3 tablespoons olive oil

½ small yellow onion, coarsely chopped

1 large clove garlic, minced

Sea salt and freshly ground pepper

1 (28-ounce) can crushed tomatoes

1 bay leaf

1 tablespoon balsamic vinegar

1 teaspoon dried oregano

Heat the olive oil in a large saucepan over medium heat. Add the onion and garlic and cook for about 3 minutes, or until the onion is translucent. Add the salt and pepper to taste, and the crushed tomatoes. Stir the ingredients together and let simmer for 1 to 2 minutes, then add the bay leaf, balsamic vinegar, and oregano and simmer for 20 minutes more. If the sauce becomes too thick, add another 1 to 2 tablespoons of water. Set aside until ready to use.

Leftover sauce may be frozen for up to three months.

Yields 3 cups sauce

Risotto with Leeks, Chard, Prosciutto, and Mascarpone

Fresh, salty, creamy, rich; what else is there to say? Pair this luscious risotto with a crisp endive salad tossed in a light lemony vinaigrette, and you're in for a real treat.

4 ounces red Swiss chard, stemmed and chopped (about 3 cups packed)

3 cups low-salt chicken broth (you may not use all of it)

3 tablespoons butter

1 tablespoon olive oil

¾ cup thinly sliced leek (white and pale green parts only)

1 cup Arborio rice

¼ cup dry white wine

2 ounces prosciutto, minced (about ¼ cup)

1½ tablespoons mascarpone cheese

1 tablespoon chopped fresh Italian parsley

Large pinch of sea salt

Pepper

Cook the Swiss chard in a pot of boiling salted water until crisp-tender, about 1 minute. Drain in a colander, then squeeze the water out with the back of a wooden spoon until dry.

Bring the broth to a boil in a medium saucepan. Reduce the heat to very low; cover and keep warm.

Meanwhile, melt the butter with the oil in a large, heavy saucepan over medium heat. Add the leeks and sauté until tender, about 5 minutes. Add the rice and stir 2 minutes. Add the wine and simmer until absorbed, stirring constantly, about 5 minutes. Add ½ cup of the hot chicken broth. Reduce the heat and simmer on medium-low until the broth is absorbed, stirring frequently. Continue adding broth, ¼ cup at a time, allowing the broth to be absorbed before adding more and stirring frequently until the rice is just tender and the mixture is creamy, about 28 to 30 minutes.

Add the chard and stir until heated through, about 2 minutes. Remove from the heat. Stir in the prosciutto, mascarpone, and parsley. Season with salt and pepper to taste and serve.

Antonia's Paella

When my mother throws dinner parties, the dish she most often prepares is paella. Her version is divine, but it takes a while to prepare and the list of ingredients is even more extensive than my abridged version below, which is just as delicious.

½ teaspoon oregano

4 black peppercorns

1 large clove garlic, coarsely chopped

¼ teaspoon salt

2 tablespoons olive oil

1 teaspoon Spanish sherry vinegar

3 chicken thighs

1 slice prosciutto or Serrano ham, cut into thin strips

¼ or ½ linguiça sausage (4- to 5-inch length), cut into disks

1 small yellow onion, coarsely chopped

½ green bell pepper, coarsely chopped

Pinch of coriander

½ teaspoon salted capers, rinsed

1 tablespoon tomato paste

1 cup long-grain rice

½ teaspoon saffron threads

6 cherrystone clams, cleaned

4 Tiger shrimp, shelled and deveined

1 cooked lobster tail, cut into large pieces (optional)

½ cup frozen petite peas

½ cup coarsely chopped fresh Italian parsley

¾ teaspoon grated and finely chopped fresh lemon zest

In a medium bowl, combine the oregano, peppercorns, garlic, salt, olive oil, and vinegar. Toss the chicken in the marinade, and marinate for 3 to 5 minutes. Remove the peppercorns.

In a medium cast-iron sauté pan over moderate heat, add the chicken and marinade and brown the chicken for 3 minutes per side. Reduce the heat to medium-low and add the ham, linguiça, onion, green pepper, coriander, and capers and sauté for 5 to 10 minutes, or until the onion is translucent. Add the tomato paste and rice and sauté for 5 minutes, then add 2¼ cups water and the saffron. Bring to a simmer, cover, and cook for 12 minutes. If the dish begins to dry out add 2 tablespoons more water.

Meanwhile, place 5 tablespoons of water in a medium saucepan over medium heat. Bring to a simmer and add the clams. Cover the pan and let steam for 10 minutes; discard any clams that do not open. Keep warm.

After the rice has cooked for 12 minutes, add the shrimp, cover, and cook for 5 minutes, then add the lobster, if using, and frozen peas and cook for an additional 2 to 3 minutes. Top with the clams and no more than 3 tablespoons of the clam juice and cook for another minute. Take the dish off the stove, sprinkle with the parsley and lemon zest, and serve.

Chicken Tagine for Two

After experimenting with a number of tagines over the years, this one keeps emerging as my favorite. Be careful—the exotic flavors of this dish may inspire your guest to perform a belly dance.

....

4 to 5 chicken thighs, skinned

3 tablespoons olive oil

1 yellow onion, thinly sliced

2 garlic cloves, finely chopped

¾ teaspoon turmeric

1 teaspoon ground ginger

1½ cups chicken stock

4 threads saffron

¼ teaspoon ground cumin

1½ tablespoons honey

1 cinnamon stick

½ cup halved dried figs

½ cup quartered dried apricots

⅓ cup whole blanched almonds

Salt and freshly ground pepper

Juice of 1 lemon

Couscous (facing page)

2 tablespoons minced fresh cilantro

Rinse the chicken thighs and pat dry with paper towels.

In a large Dutch oven or tagine (10 to 12 inches wide), heat 2 tablespoons of the olive oil over medium heat until almost smoking. Add the chicken and brown on both sides for 4 to 5 minutes. Remove and set aside.

Add the remaining 1 tablespoon of olive oil, the onions, and the garlic to the pot and sauté for 2 to 3 minutes. Return the chicken to the pot and add the turmeric, ginger, stock, saffron, and cumin. Reduce the heat to medium-low and cook uncovered for 55 minutes, stirring occasionally, or until the meat is nearly falling off the bone.

While the chicken is cooking, combine the honey, cinnamon, and ½ cup water in a small saucepan and bring to a boil. Add the figs and apricots. Reduce the liquid to a simmer and cook until the fruit is tender and the liquid has reduced to a syrupy glaze, about 15 minutes, adding more water if the pan gets dry. Discard the cinnamon stick.

Preheat the oven to broil. Arrange a rack on the middle shelf of the oven.

Spread the almonds on a pie plate, set on the middle of the rack, and toast in the oven, watching carefully, until golden brown, 3 to 4 minutes. Remove from the oven and set aside.

Season the chicken mixture with salt and pepper to taste, then stir in the lemon juice and the fruit syrup.

Serve over the couscous and sprinkle with the toasted almonds and cilantro.

Couscous

1½ tablespoons unsalted butter   ½ teaspoon salt   1 cup instant couscous

In a medium saucepan, combine 1 cup water with the butter and salt. Bring to a boil. Remove from the heat and stir in the couscous. Cover the pan and let stand for 6 minutes, or until the water is absorbed and the grains fluffy.

Remove the lid and fluff with a fork. Serve warm.

Split Chicken Breast Puttanesca Style
with Green Olives, Tomatoes, Onions, Thyme, and Lemon Zest

Sure, you could have zesty, savory puttanesca sauce over pasta, but why not jazz up a chicken dinner instead? If you would like the dish to have a little kick, add a large pinch of red pepper flakes.

1 tablespoon olive oil

½ large yellow onion, coarsely chopped

2 garlic cloves, sliced

¼ teaspoon sea salt

1½ cups canned whole plum tomatoes, drained

1 boneless, skinless chicken breast (split)

1 tablespoon capers

1 cup green olives, pitted

1 teaspoon fresh thyme leaves

1 teaspoon grated and finely chopped fresh lemon zest

5 anchovy fillets, coarsely chopped

Salt and pepper

In a large nonreactive sauté pan over medium heat, heat the olive oil for 30 seconds. Add the onions and sauté until translucent, about 3 to 5 minutes. Add the garlic and salt and sauté for another 2 minutes. Add the tomatoes and mash into pieces with a spoon or fork. Cook for 5 minutes.

Add the chicken, capers, olives, thyme, lemon zest, and anchovies. Stir the sauce around, spooning it over the chicken until it is covered in the sauce. Cover the chicken and cook for 5 to 7 minutes per side (depending on thickness); when done, the chicken breast should be white and juicy and its juices should run clear when pierced with a knife. Don't overcook the chicken or it will become chewy. Season with salt and pepper to taste and serve.

Lamb Shanks Braised in Red Wine with Baby Carrots, Cipollini Onions, and Fingerling Potatoes

The meat is so succulent and soft in this dish that you'll want to eat it with a spoon. Pair this with a crisp green salad and warm, crunchy French bread, and you'll be a happy, sated couple.

2 tablespoons olive oil

2 lamb shanks (about 1½ pounds)

1 large clove garlic, minced

1 (12- to 14-ounce) can chopped tomatoes in their juices

½ teaspoon grated and finely chopped fresh orange zest

½ teaspoon dried marjoram, crumbled

1 bay leaf

1½ cups dry red wine

6 cipollini onions, peeled

8 baby carrots

10 to 12 fingerling potatoes, washed

Sea salt and freshly ground pepper

1 tablespoon minced fresh Italian parsley

Preheat the oven to 375°F.

Heat 1 tablespoon of the olive oil in a large sauté pan over medium-high heat. Brown the lamb shanks on both sides, turning occasionally, and cooking for 8 to 10 minutes. Remove the lamb from the pan, and set aside.

In a 9-quart heavy Dutch oven over medium heat, add the remaining tablespoon of olive oil, then add the garlic and sauté until translucent. Add the lamb, tomatoes, orange zest, marjoram, bay leaf, and ¾ cup of the wine. Bring to a simmer and let the flavors meld, continuing to cook, for 10 minutes.

Cover the pot and place it in the oven. After 30 minutes, add the cipollini onions, carrots, and fingerling potatoes, cover, and cook for another 30 minutes. Add the remaining ¾ cup of red wine and cook for an additional 30 to 40 minutes.

Pull the casserole from the oven and season with salt and pepper to taste. Distribute the shanks and vegetables among two large plates. Spoon the juices over the top and garnish with the parsley.

Szechuan-Style Stir-Fried Steak with Peppers, Onions, and Snow Peas over Noodles

Fast and fabulous—that's the best way I can describe this dish. You certainly can substitute other vegetables such as broccoli florets, asparagus, and green beans. Just be sure to keep them slightly crisp, but not raw.

2 tablespoons canola oil

1 pound boneless sirloin steak, cut into 3-by-¼-by-¼-inch strips

2 tablespoons soy sauce

½ teaspoon hoisin or plum sauce

½ teaspoon cornstarch

¼ teaspoon red pepper flakes

6 ounces dried udon noodles

2 teaspoons sesame oil

2 large cloves garlic, sliced

1 large yellow onion, sliced into thin rings, then halved

½ red bell pepper, seeded and cut vertically into ¼-inch slices

½ yellow bell pepper, seeded and cut vertically into ¼-inch slices

1 cup snow peas, stemmed

2 teaspoons minced fresh cilantro

Heat 1 tablespoon of the canola oil in a large sauté pan over medium-high heat until sizzling. Add the steak and stir-fry until browned but still pink inside, about 4 minutes. With a slotted spoon, transfer the steak strips to a plate.

In a small bowl, combine the soy sauce, hoisin sauce, cornstarch, 5 tablespoons water, and the red pepper flakes. Stir until the sauce is smooth.

Fill a medium stockpot with water. When the water boils, cook the noodles according to the package directions. Drain and toss with 1 teaspoon of the sesame oil.

In the same sauté pan you used to cook the beef, heat the remaining tablespoon of canola oil and teaspoon of sesame oil for 1 minute over medium heat. Add the garlic and sauté for 1 to 2 minutes or until soft, then add the onions, red peppers, yellow peppers, snow peas, and 2 tablespoons water. Cook for 3 minutes, or until the vegetables are beginning to soften but are still crisp. Add the steak to the mixture and cook for 3 to 4 minutes, then add the sauce and stir-fry the vegetables and steak for an additional minute or until completely coated with the sauce.

Divide the udon noodles between two large dinner plates. Cover the noodles with the stir-fry, drizzle any extra sauce over the top, garnish with cilantro, and serve.

ROMANTIC MEALS

Poached Eggs with Prosciutto and Heirloom Tomatoes, Drizzled with Basil Oil, PAGE 63

Two Pizzas with Two Toppings: Broccoli Rabe, Goat and Fontina Cheese, Toasted Pine Nuts, and Currants; Fresh Mozzarella, Caramelized Onions, and Thyme, PAGE 64

Homemade Ricotta Gnocchi with Orange, Sage, and Brown Butter Sauce and a Watercress and Blood Orange Salad, PAGE 66

Frittata with Goat Cheese, Baby Zucchini, Prosciutto, and Cherry Tomatoes, PAGE 68

Poached Black Cod in Ginger-Miso Broth with Frizzled Leeks, PAGE 69

Split Broiled Lobster with Lime Butter and Celery Root Remoulade, PAGE 70

Steamed Halibut Packages with Pan-Seared Cherry Tomatoes and Garlicky Haricots Verts, PAGE 73

Seared Scallops on a Bed of Fresh English Pea and Mint Purée, PAGE 74

Crispy Trout with Herbal Salsa and Baby Tomato Relish, PAGE 77

Cornish Game Hens Stuffed with Sweet Italian Sausage, Prunes, and Savory with Cinnamon Butternut Squash, PAGE 78

Steak au Poivre with Minted Sugar Snap Peas, PAGE 80

Mini Rack of Lamb with Nutty Beluga Lentils and Sautéed Garlic Spinach, PAGE 83

SUGGESTED DRINKS

Campari and soda, Lillet, dry Champagne, or nonalcoholic Ginger Limeade (divide juice of 4 limes, 2 tablespoons superfine sugar, and ¼ teaspoon finely minced fresh ginger between two glasses filled three-fourths with sparkling water or seltzer)

Poached Eggs with Prosciutto and Heirloom Tomatoes, Drizzled with Basil Oil

Serve this runny, gooey, divine breakfast on a nutty, grainy piece of toast. You'll want to make a habit of this perfect breakfast combination.

2 tablespoons finely minced fresh basil

¼ cup olive oil

Sea salt and freshly ground pepper

1 large heirloom tomato (such as Purple Cherokee), sliced into disks

4 thin slices prosciutto

3 tablespoons white or rice vinegar

4 large eggs

Place the basil in a blender, pulse, and then with the blender running slowly add the olive oil. When it's completely blended, add salt and pepper to taste. Pour the basil oil into a small pitcher, and set aside.

Arrange 2 to 3 slices of tomato in the middle of two large dinner plates. Cover the tomatoes with 2 slices of prosciutto.

Fill a large skillet with 1½ to 2 inches of water and place over medium heat until the water comes to a low simmer, then add the vinegar. Wait for 1 minute, then add the eggs by cracking each into a bowl and carefully slipping each egg into the water. Let the eggs cook for 4 minutes. If the yolks still look too runny for your liking, spoon some water on top of the eggs and cook for another 30 seconds. Remove the eggs carefully from the water with a slotted spoon.

Place 2 eggs on top of each tomato-prosciutto bed. Drizzle the basil oil lightly over the top of the eggs. Sprinkle with a pinch of salt, and serve.

Two Pizzas with Two Toppings: Broccoli Rabe, Goat and Fontina Cheese, Toasted Pine Nuts, and Currants; Fresh Mozzarella, Caramelized Onions, and Thyme

Once you've had these delightful pizzas you'll never want to order out again! As soon as you've mastered the crust, feel free to invent your own toppings—anything goes.

DOUGH

1 package active dry yeast

¾ cup warm water (around 110°F)

1 tablespoon olive oil, plus extra for the bowl

1½ cups all-purpose flour, plus extra for kneading

1 teaspoon salt

¼ cup cornmeal

TOPPINGS

½ teaspoon salt

½ head broccoli rabe, 1 inch cut off the stems, halved

3 tablespoons pine nuts

3 tablespoons currants

2 tablespoons olive oil

1½ large yellow onions, thinly sliced

1 small jar marinated artichokes, drained

½ cup crumbled goat cheese

½ cup shredded Italian fontina cheese

1 large ball (about 3½ ounces) fresh mozzarella, thinly sliced

4 sprigs fresh thyme

FOR THE DOUGH: In a small bowl, whisk together the yeast, warm water, and olive oil. Let the mixture stand for 3 to 5 minutes while the yeast activates and becomes foamy. If the yeast does not foam, throw it out and begin again; otherwise the dough will not rise. In a large bowl, mix together the flour and salt. Slowly add the yeast mixture to the flour, folding them together with a rubber spatula until the dough barely comes together.

Turn the dough out onto a clean surface dusted with flour and knead it until it becomes elastic and completely smooth, about 8 to 10 minutes. The dough is ready when you push it with your finger and it bounces back. Grease a large bowl with olive oil and place the dough inside, cover the bowl with plastic wrap or a

dishtowel, and put in a warm place. Let it rise for 1 to 2 hours, or until doubled in size.

Preheat the oven to 425°F.

Punch the dough down and divide it into two pieces, cover each with a kitchen towel, and let stand for 30 minutes.

FOR THE TOPPINGS: Fill a stockpot halfway with water and bring to a boil. Add the salt and the broccoli rabe and cook for 6 to 8 minutes or until soft. Drain completely.

Spread the pine nuts on a pie tin and place on a rack set on the upper shelf of the oven. Watching carefully, toast for 3 to 4 minutes or until golden brown. Transfer to paper towels and let cool for 10 minutes.

Place the currants in a small ovenproof bowl and cover with boiling water. Let stand for 20 minutes, or until plump. Drain and set aside.

In a medium sauté pan, heat the olive oil for 1 to 2 minutes. Add the onions and sauté 10 to 15 minutes more, stirring occasionally, or until soft and deep amber brown. Remove to a bowl.

On a floured surface, begin to knead each ball of dough, one at a time: Take the ball and with the palm of your hand, push the dough away from you, then continue around and around in a circle until you have a flattened circular crust. The crust should feel smooth.

Spread the cornmeal evenly on 2 pizza sheets (or baking sheets), then place the rounds of pizza dough on top. Bake for 6 to 8 minutes or until golden. Pull from the oven and top one pizza with the broccoli rabe, pine nuts, currants, artichokes, and goat and fontina cheeses; top the other with the caramelized onions and mozzarella cheese. Drizzle each pizza with olive oil and bake for another 8 to 10 minutes, or until the cheese is melted and bubbly. Place thyme on top of the mozzarella and carmelized onion pizza for garnish. Serve immediately.

Homemade Ricotta Gnocchi
with **Orange, Sage,** and **Brown Butter Sauce**
and a **Watercress** and **Blood Orange Salad**

Gnocchi are usually made from cooked potatoes and flour, and though they are one of my favorite Italian dishes, if made incorrectly, they can be leaden and heavy. Here's a lighter method for making a different kind of gnocchi that is delicious and foolproof. To enjoy leftover gnocchi, heat 1 tablespoon of olive oil and 1 teaspoon of water in a small skillet. Add the gnocchi, cover, and cook 1 to 2 minutes to heat through. Toss with chopped, fresh tomatoes and herbs as desired.

2 cups fresh whole-milk ricotta cheese, drained in a sieve for 2 to 3 hours

1 ⅓ cups freshly grated Parmesan

2 large eggs

¼ cup all-purpose flour

½ teaspoon salt, plus more to taste

Freshly grated nutmeg

2 tablespoons olive oil

2 teaspoons balsamic vinegar

2 bunches watercress, cleaned and stemmed

½ teaspoon grated and finely chopped fresh blood orange zest, plus the peeled and sliced segments from 1 blood orange (about 12 to 16 sections)

Pepper to taste

4 tablespoons unsalted butter

10 fresh sage leaves

In a large bowl, combine the ricotta, Parmesan, eggs, and flour. Add the salt and nutmeg and mix until a soft dough forms.

Turn the dough out onto a floured surface. Roll the dough into two long 14- to 16-inch ropes (each about 1 inch in diameter); sprinkle with flour if the dough is too sticky. Cut each rope into 18 to 20 pieces. Press the tines of a fork into each piece to create an indentation. Arrange the finished gnocchi on a piece of parchment or waxed paper next to the stove.

In a medium bowl, whisk together the olive oil and balsamic vinegar. Add the watercress and blood orange segments. Toss until the leaves and oranges are coated in the dressing. Season with pepper, to taste.

Bring a medium pot of water to a boil. Add the gnocchi in two batches, cooking each batch for 5 to 6 minutes or until they begin to expand and rise to the surface of the water.

In a medium saucepan, melt 1 tablespoon of the butter, then add the sage leaves and let brown for 2 to 3 minutes, or until crispy. Set the leaves aside to drain on a paper towel.

Melt the remaining 3 tablespoons of butter in the same saucepan. Add the blood orange zest to the butter and continue to cook the butter until it is light brown, about 2 to 3 minutes. Add the cooked gnocchi to the sauce, carefully spooning the sauce over them.

On two large dinner plates place a large pillow of greens dotted with the blood oranges, and next to them place 10 to 12 of the gnocchi. Drizzle the gnocchi with the brown butter and garnish with the crispy sage leaves, then serve.

Frittata with Goat Cheese, Baby Zucchini, Prosciutto, and Cherry Tomatoes

This frittata is a favorite in my house. The blend of salty, sweet, and earthy flavors makes every bite completely satisfying. It's perfect to serve for a Saturday or Sunday breakfast or brunch. Serve it with corn muffins (page 44).

4 large eggs

¼ cup heavy cream

4 teaspoons olive oil

4 to 6 baby zucchini, ends removed and thinly sliced lengthwise

6 cherry tomatoes, halved

1 teaspoon minced fresh thyme

3 tablespoons goat cheese, cut into bite-size pieces

2 slices prosciutto, torn into bite-size pieces

Sea salt and freshly ground pepper

Preheat the oven to 375°F.

In a medium bowl, crack the eggs, then add the cream. Whisk the eggs until they are fully beaten and slightly fluffy.

Lightly grease the interior of a medium cast-iron frying pan with 1 teaspoon of olive oil, then heat the remaining 3 teaspoons of olive oil over medium-low heat for 1 minute. Add the zucchini and sauté for 2 to 3 minutes. Add the tomatoes and thyme and cook for 2 to 3 minutes more, stirring continuously. Add the egg mixture and cook for 4 minutes more, or until set. Sprinkle the eggs with the goat cheese, prosciutto, and salt and pepper to taste.

Place the frittata in the oven and bake until puffy and golden, about 15 minutes.

Poached Black Cod in Ginger-Miso Broth
with Frizzled Leeks

I like to serve this dish on a bed of jasmine rice or soba noodles. That way you maximize your chances of getting every last drop of the broth.

1 tablespoon canola oil

2 tablespoons sesame oil

2 to 3 leeks, cleaned well, white parts only, cut into ¼-inch disks

3 large cloves garlic, sliced

2 ½ tablespoons minced fresh ginger

¼ cup sake

¼ cup mirin

¼ cup white miso paste

1 tablespoon soy sauce

Two 8-ounce black cod fillets

3 tablespoons fresh cilantro

In a medium sauté pan, heat the canola oil and 1 tablespoon of the sesame oil until sizzling, about 2 minutes. Add the leeks and sauté until they are wilted, then crisped and golden on the edges, at least 15 minutes; if browning too quickly, add a tablespoon or two of water to the pan. Remove the leeks from the pan and drain on paper towels.

In a large, heavy sauté pan, add the remaining 1 tablespoon sesame oil and heat for 1 minute over medium heat. Add the garlic and ginger to the pan, sauté for 2 to 3 minutes, then add the sake, mirin, miso paste, soy sauce, and 1½ cups water. Turn down the heat and mix the miso paste into the liquid until fully dissolved. Place the cod fillets in the broth, spoon the liquid over the fish, cover, and cook for 10 to 15 minutes, or until the fish flakes easily.

Place the fillets in shallow soup bowls and spoon the broth over the fish to cover. Sprinkle with the frizzled leeks and fresh cilantro and serve.

Split Broiled Lobster with Lime Butter and Celery Root Remoulade

You won't be able to find a more decadent dinner that's easier than this one. I get the lobster at a fish store where it's been cooked, split, and cleaned. I use Pacific lobster because I live on the West Coast, but an Eastern lobster tail would work beautifully, too.

2 lobsters, cooked, split, and cleaned

5 tablespoons unsalted butter

2 cloves garlic, sliced

½ cup breadcrumbs

1 tablespoon finely chopped fresh Italian parsley

Salt and pepper

Juice of 1 lime

Celery Root Remoulade (facing page)

Preheat the oven to broil.

Place the lobsters flesh side up on a baking sheet.

In a small sauté pan, melt 2 tablespoons of the butter. Add the garlic and sauté over medium-low heat until just translucent, about 3 minutes. Throw in the breadcrumbs and brown for 1 to 2 minutes. Add the parsley and salt and pepper to taste.

Spoon the breadcrumbs into the cavity of the lobster.

In a small saucepan, melt the remaining 3 tablespoons butter with the lime juice. Drizzle the lobsters with the melted butter, and place under the broiler for 30 seconds to brown.

Place 2 lobster halves on the sides of 2 large dinner plates, with a large scoop of the Celery Root Remoulade in the center.

Celery Root Remoulade

¼ cup mayonnaise

3 tablespoons finely chopped fresh
Italian parsley

1 tablespoon Dijon mustard

1 teaspoon fresh lemon juice

Salt and freshly cracked pepper

One 12-ounce celery root, peeled

In a medium bowl, combine the mayonnaise, parsley, mustard, lemon juice, and salt and pepper to taste.

Cut the celery root in half and then into quarters. Make sure the size of the chunks can fit into a food processor (if you don't have a food processor, cut the root into matchstick pieces). The food processor should be fitted with a shredding blade.

Shred the celery root, then transfer it to the sauce. Toss the celery root until it is coated in the dressing and soft, and add more salt and pepper if needed.

Steamed Halibut Packages with Pan-Seared Cherry Tomatoes and Garlicky Haricots Verts

I adore this method of cooking fish because the flesh stays so soft and tender. If you want to change the fish or vegetables in the package, any meaty fish does well, and zucchini and thinly sliced leeks also work well.

Two 12-ounce halibut steaks

3 paper-thin slices red onion

Six ¼-inch-thick slices fennel

4 stems fresh thyme

4 paper-thin slices lemon

6 tablespoons olive oil

½ cup white wine

½ pound haricots verts

3 cloves garlic, sliced

1 cup cherry tomatoes

Salt and freshly ground pepper

Preheat the oven to 400°F.

Place a large piece of foil on a baking sheet and put the fish in the center of the foil. Roll the sides of the foil up so that they act as a container for the liquids. Combine the onion slices and fennel slices, and place them on top of the fish. Scatter the thyme and lemon slices over the top. Drizzle 2 tablespoons of olive oil and ¼ cup of white wine over the top of each steak. Fold the foil around the fish into a neat package, leaving some air between the top of the foil and the fish.

Place the pan in the oven and cook for 17 minutes. Check to see if the fish is cooked through, and if not, close the foil and return to the oven for 2 to 3 more minutes. Fish is touchy, so err on the side of undercooking so it doesn't become dry.

While the fish is cooking, add an inch or two of water to a steamer and bring to a boil. Throw in the haricots verts, cover, and steam for 2 to 3 minutes or until crisp but tender.

In a medium sauté pan add 1 tablespoon of olive oil and the garlic over medium heat and cook until translucent, about 3 minutes. Turn the heat to high, add the haricots verts, and sauté for 1 minute. Arrange the haricots verts on two dinner plates.

In the same sauté pan, add the remaining 1 tablespoon of olive oil and heat for 1 minute. Turn the heat to high and add the tomatoes, tossing them in the pan. Let them sear for 3 to 4 minutes, stirring occasionally, then place next to the haricots verts.

Open the foil packages and place the two steaks next to the vegetables, then lightly drizzle the fish with the juices.

Add a dusting of salt and freshly ground pepper to the dish, and serve.

Seared Scallops on a Bed of Fresh English Pea and Mint Purée

The brilliant green purée topped with the light amber scallops looks like a fabulous abstract painting. The buttery scallops go very well with the sweet, fresh flavors of the minty pea purée.

2 cups fresh or frozen English peas

2 tablespoons coarsely chopped fresh mint

1 clove garlic, coarsely chopped

¼ teaspoon salt

Freshly ground pepper

3 tablespoons butter

1 teaspoon fresh lemon juice

Large pinch of paprika

12 large sea scallops (about 12 ounces)

Fill a small saucepan with a couple of inches of water. Bring to a boil, add the peas, and cook until tender, about 3 to 5 minutes for fresh peas, about 1 minute for frozen peas. Place the peas in a blender and add the mint, garlic, salt, and pepper to taste. Blend until smooth. Place the pea purée in the saucepan to keep warm.

In a medium-heavy sauté pan (preferably cast iron), heat the butter over medium-high heat.

Add the lemon juice and paprika. When the butter begins to foam, add the scallops. Cook for 2 minutes per side or until just cooked through and each side is golden to amber brown on top.

Spoon the pea purée into two shallow soup dishes, creating a bed, then place the seared scallops on top and serve.

Crispy Trout with Herbal Salsa and Baby Tomato Relish

Make sure to get the skin of the trout as crispy as possible, and please don't shy away from eating it—it's delicious! If you're a fan of cherry tomatoes, double the recipe for the tomato relish, because you'll want to keep spooning it on.

Juice of 1 lemon

1 tablespoon olive oil

1 teaspoon coarsely chopped fresh Italian parsley

1 teaspoon coarsely chopped fresh mint

1 teaspoon coarsely chopped fresh basil

½ teaspoon chopped fresh thyme leaves

1 cup cherry or Sweet 100 tomatoes, halved

1 tablespoon minced shallot or red onion

1 tablespoon balsamic vinegar

⅛ teaspoon salt, plus more to taste

¼ teaspoon freshly ground pepper, plus more to taste

Two 10- to 12-ounce whole brook trout

½ cup all-purpose flour

3 tablespoons unsalted butter

In a medium bowl, combine the lemon juice, olive oil, and fresh herbs and mix until completely blended. Set aside.

In another medium bowl, combine the tomatoes, shallot, and balsamic vinegar, and toss. Season with salt and pepper. Set aside.

Rinse the trout and pat dry. On a large plate mix the flour, the ⅛ teaspoon salt, and the ¼ teaspoon pepper together. Dredge the trout in the flour mixture. In a large, heavy pan (preferably cast iron), heat the butter over medium-high heat until melted and just beginning to brown, about 3 to 4 minutes. Place the trout in the butter and cook for 4 minutes per side, or until crispy on the outside and opaque in the center.

Arrange the trout on two large dinner plates. Top with the herbal salsa and tomato relish, and serve.

Cornish Game Hens Stuffed with Sweet Italian Sausage, Prunes, and Savory with Cinnamon Butternut Squash

I like to refer to this recipe as a mini Thanksgiving—if you're missing all the flavors of Turkey Day, but want it to be manageable for two, this is your meal.

2 Cornish game hens (1¼ pounds each)

2 teaspoons olive oil, plus more for coating the hens

¼ cup yellow onion, coarsely chopped

1 celery stalk, tough fibers removed and coarsely chopped

2 large Italian sausages, casing removed

1 tablespoon coarsely chopped fresh Italian parsley

2 teaspoons fresh winter or summer savory, whole or coarsely chopped (or 1 teaspoon dried)

¼ cup coarsely chopped pitted prunes

½ cup dried breadcrumbs

½ cup hot chicken stock

1 teaspoon freshly grated and finely chopped orange zest

Salt and pepper

2 tablespoons unsalted butter

4 teaspoons dark brown sugar

⅛ teaspoon cinnamon

⅛ teaspoon nutmeg

1 butternut squash, halved and seeded

Preheat the oven to 400°F.

Wash and dry the game hens. Place them on a rack inside a roasting pan.

Heat the 2 teaspoons of olive oil in a large sauté pan over medium-high heat, then add the onion and celery and sauté until translucent, about 3 to 4 minutes. Add the Italian sausage and cook, crumbling the sausage, for about 6 minutes, or until cooked through.

Place the sausage mixture in a medium bowl and stir in the parsley, savory, prunes, and breadcrumbs. Add the hot chicken stock slowly, blending as you go. Finish the stuffing by blending in the orange zest and salt and pepper to taste.

Fill the hens with the stuffing. Truss the cavity tightly with a skewer or kitchen twine. Rub the outside of the birds with olive oil, and salt and pepper, and place them on the upper rack of the oven.

In a small bowl, combine the butter, brown sugar, cinnamon, and nutmeg, and season with salt and pepper to taste. Place the squash on a baking sheet, spoon the brown sugar mixture into the squash cavity, and place on the bottom rack of the oven.

Cook the hens for 1 hour, or until the juices run clear when pierced with a knife and the meat is completely opaque; a thermometer should read 160°F when inserted into the thigh. Cook the squash at the same time, for 1 hour, or until the squash is soft when pricked with a fork, and golden on top.

Steak au Poivre with Minted Sugar Snap Peas

This French classic is terribly elegant without a bit of fuss. I like to serve it with crisp sugar snap peas and mint to lighten the rich, dense flavors of the meat and sauce, while at the same time enhancing them.

2 boneless beef top loin (strip) steaks, ¾ to 1 inch thick and 8 to 10 ounces each

2 teaspoons kosher salt

1 tablespoon whole black peppercorns

2 teaspoons olive oil

¼ cup finely chopped shallots

1 tablespoon unsalted butter, cut into 2 pieces

¼ cup cognac or other brandy

¼ cup heavy cream

Minted Sugar Snap Peas (facing page)

Preheat the oven to 200°F.

Rinse the steaks and pat dry. Season both sides with kosher salt.

Coarsely crush the peppercorns in a sealed plastic bag with a meat pounder or the bottom of a heavy skillet, then press the pepper evenly onto both sides of the steaks.

Heat a 12-inch heavy skillet (preferably cast iron) over moderately high heat until hot, about 3 minutes, then add the oil, swirling to coat the skillet, and sauté the steaks, turning over once, 2 to 3 minutes per side, 6 minutes total for medium-rare.

Transfer the steaks to a heatproof platter and keep warm in the oven while making the sauce.

Pour off the fat from the skillet, add the shallots and butter, and cook over moderately low heat, stirring and scraping up the brown bits, until the shallots are translucent and well browned all over, 3 to 4 minutes.

Add the cognac (use caution; it may ignite) and bring to a boil. Reduce the heat and stir until the liquid is reduced to a glaze, 2 to 3 minutes. Add the cream and any meat juices accumulated on the platter and boil the sauce, stirring occasionally, until reduced by half, about 2 minutes. Pour the sauce over the steaks and serve with the Minted Sugar Snap Peas.

Minted Sugar Snap Peas

You won't be able to resist grabbing a sugar snap pea or two while preparing this savory side dish.

6 to 8 ounces sugar snap peas, stems and strings removed

2 teaspoons olive oil

2 tablespoons coarsely chopped fresh mint

Salt and freshly cracked pepper

Add ½ cup of water to a vegetable steamer and bring it to a boil. Add the snap peas and cook for 2 to 3 minutes, or until just tender. Rinse in cold water.

In a medium saucepan, heat the olive oil until sizzling. Add the snap peas and stir for 30 seconds or until coated. Add the mint and salt and pepper to taste, stir several times until coated, and serve.

Mini Rack of Lamb with Nutty Beluga Lentils and Sautéed Garlic Spinach

The three main elements in this recipe make an unbeatable combination. The soft, sweet taste of the lamb coupled with the full green flavor of the spinach and the nutty, full-bodied taste of the lentils makes every bite a gastronomic pleasure. These lentils are one of my favorites. Here I've interpreted a recipe from the masterful chef Judy Rodgers of San Francisco's Zuni Café.

3½ tablespoons olive oil

½ yellow onion, finely chopped

½ medium carrot, finely chopped

½ stalk celery, tough fibers removed and finely chopped

1 cup Beluga lentils (or French green lentils)

1 bay leaf

1 cup red wine

2 cups chicken stock

Sea salt and pepper

1 pound (4-rib) Frenched rack of lamb, trimmed of all but a thin layer of fat

1 tablespoon finely chopped fresh rosemary

3 large cloves garlic, sliced

4 cups washed and torn spinach

Preheat the oven to 375°F.

In a medium sauté pan, heat 1½ tablespoons of the olive oil for 1 minute over medium heat. Add the onion, carrot, and celery, and sauté the vegetables until they are softened, 5 to 7 minutes. Add the lentils and bay leaf and sauté for 3 minutes more, coating all the lentils. Increase the heat and add the red wine. Bring to a simmer and cook uncovered, stirring, until the mixture becomes dry. Meanwhile, in a saucepan bring the chicken stock to a simmer, then turn off the heat and cover to keep warm. Add the warm chicken stock to the lentils (like cooking risotto) ½ cup at a time, letting the lentils absorb the liquid with each addition. Repeat, stirring the mixture constantly. After 28 to 30 minutes the lentils should be slightly chewy and tender. Season to taste with salt and pepper.

While the lentils are cooking, rinse and pat the lamb dry and rub it with 1 tablespoon of the olive oil. Season the meat with salt and pepper, then press the rosemary into the flesh.

Place the lamb in a small roasting pan in the middle of the oven, and roast for 30 to 35 minutes, or until a thermometer inserted in the thickest part of the meat registers 140°F.

While both the lentils and the meat are cooking, prepare the spinach. In a medium sauté pan, heat the remaining 1 tablespoon of olive oil for 1 minute over medium heat. Add the garlic and sauté until just translucent but not brown. Add the spinach and sauté for 2 minutes, then cover and cook for an additional 2 minutes, or until completely wilted. Season to taste with salt and pepper.

Slice the rack in half. On two large dinner plates, arrange a bed of lentils and a side of spinach, then place the lamb on top of the lentils and serve.

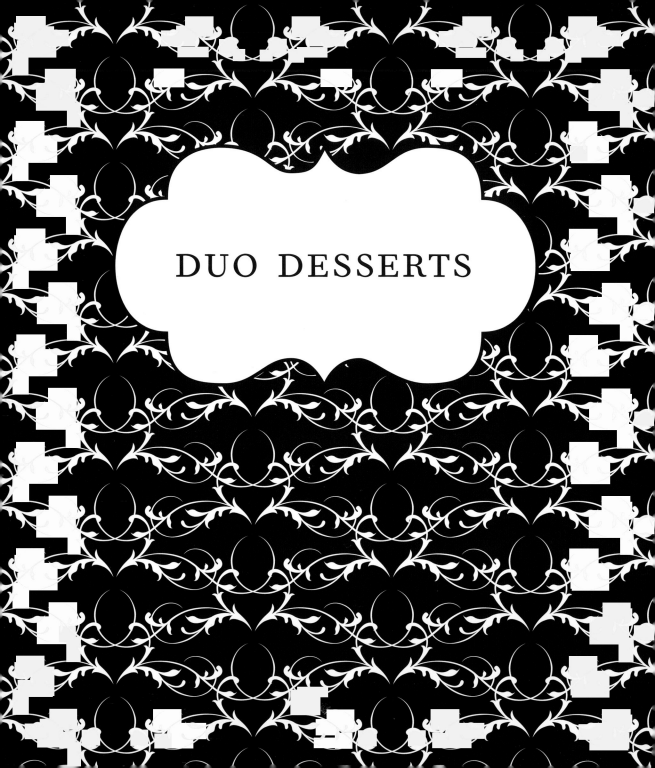

DUO DESSERTS

SUGGESTED DRINKS

Espresso with a twist of lemon rind, tawny port,
or Champagne

Mixed Berry Shortcakes
with Crème Fraîche Whipped Cream

Shortcakes are an old-fashioned dessert that's always in fashion, and with the slightly tart crème fraîche whipped cream, these are truly a slice—well, let's call it a bowl—of heaven.

SHORTCAKES

1 cup all-purpose flour

1 tablespoon sugar, plus 1 teaspoon

½ tablespoon baking soda

⅛ teaspoon salt

4 tablespoons cold unsalted butter, cut into ½-inch pieces

1 large egg

⅛ cup buttermilk

⅛ cup heavy cream

FILLING

½ cup strawberries, hulled and quartered

½ cup raspberries

¼ cup blackberries

¼ cup blueberries

2 tablespoons sugar

Crème Fraîche Whipped Cream (page 88)

FOR THE SHORTCAKES: Preheat the oven to 450°F.

In a food processor, mix the flour, sugar, baking soda, and salt. Add the butter a little at a time and pulse until the mixture resembles coarse crumbs, no more than 5 to 10 seconds.

In a small bowl, whisk together the egg, buttermilk, and cream, then add to the food processor. Pulse 5 to 10 times, or until the pastry just begins to hold together. (Be careful not to overmix.)

Place the dough on a floured surface and knead 5 to 6 times, just so it comes together. Shape into a round 1 inch thick, then cut the round like cutting a pie into 3 equal triangles.

Place the triangles on a greased baking sheet and bake in the oven on the bottom rack for 15 to 17 minutes, or until slightly browned and firm to touch. Transfer to a wire rack to cool.

FOR THE FILLING: In a medium bowl, combine all the berries and sugar and mix thoroughly, then let stand for 10 minutes.

Cut the shortcakes in half horizontally and place the bottoms in 2 shallow bowls. Spoon the berries over the top, then the Crème Fraîche Whipped Cream, and place the top biscuit directly on top or to the side. The extra shortcake may be stored in an airtight plastic container for up to 24 hours.

Crème Fraîche Whipped Cream

1 cup heavy cream   **3 tablespoons crème fraîche**

Blend the heavy cream and crème fraîche
using a handheld mixer or eggbeater until
soft peaks form.

Mexican Chocolate Sorbet with Bittersweet Nibs

I'm a big fan of Mexican hot chocolate, which was clearly my inspiration for this super chocolatey, cinnamon-spiked dessert. It's delicious served with a crispy wafer cookie.

¼ cup sugar

¼ cup unsweetened cocoa powder

2 whole cloves

1 cinnamon stick

¼ cup cacao nibs or mini bittersweet chocolate chips

In a medium saucepan over medium heat, combine ½ cup water with the sugar until dissolved. Whisk in the cocoa, then add the cloves and cinnamon. Simmer for 3 to 4 minutes, stirring constantly.

Remove from the stove and refrigerate for at least 2 hours.

Strain the chocolate mixture through a fine-meshed sieve into a bowl, then pour into an ice cream maker and follow the manufacturer's instructions.

When the mixture is nearly ready, add the chocolate nibs or mini-chips, and continue mixing until frozen. Serve immediately, or for a firmer consistency, place in a freezer-safe container and freeze for several hours.

90 • COOKING *for* TWO

Crystallized Ginger
and Fallen Chocolate Soufflés

This recipe was inspired by a soufflé that I once had at Restaurant Garibaldi in Oakland, California. Over time, I've made it my own by adding a few things, including crystallized ginger, which complements the chocolate beautifully.

....

2 ounces bittersweet chocolate, finely chopped

4 tablespoons unsalted butter, cut into 1-inch slices

4 tablespoons sugar

Pinch of salt

1 large egg, separated

½ teaspoon vanilla extract

Pinch of cream of tartar

1 teaspoon diced candied ginger

1 cup heavy cream, whipped

Preheat the oven to 375°F.

In a double boiler over medium-low heat, combine the chocolate, butter, 2 tablespoons of the sugar, and the salt, and cook until the chocolate is melted and smooth, stirring frequently. Remove from the heat and let cool briefly, then whisk in the egg yolk and vanilla.

Using a handheld mixer on high speed, beat the egg white and cream of tartar until soft peaks form. Add the remaining 2 tablespoons sugar and continue beating on high speed until stiff and glossy. Fold a spoonful of the egg white mixture into the chocolate batter to lighten, add the candied ginger, then fold the chocolate batter back into the whites until just combined.

Divide the batter between two 12-ounce ramekins; the batter will not fill them completely. (The soufflés can be prepared up to 24 hours ahead of time, then covered and refrigerated.)

Place the soufflés in the oven and bake until puffed and crusty, about 20 to 25 minutes. Add the whipped cream and serve warm. The soufflés will fall as they cool.

Semisweet Chocolate Fondue
with Fresh Mangoes, Strawberries, Dried Figs, Papaya, and Walnuts

I don't want to sound like a food snob, but the quality of the chocolate really matters in this dessert since it's the main ingredient. Feel free to dip whatever fruit or nut you love into the chocolate. But I can promise you that the variety below is truly divine!

⅓ cup heavy cream

8 ounces top-quality bittersweet chocolate, finely chopped

1 tablespoon Grand Marnier

1 mango, peeled, pitted, and sliced into 1-inch pieces

6 strawberries, hulled

6 dried Mission figs

½ papaya, peeled, seeded, and cut into 1-inch pieces

6 walnut, halves

Bring the cream to a simmer in a medium saucepan over low heat. Slowly whisk in the chocolate, add the Grand Marnier, and continue to whisk until completely blended.

Transfer to a fondue pot or a heated enamel dish. Arrange the fruits and nuts on a decorative plate, and serve.

Meyer Lemon Pot-au-Crème

I know this is a cookbook for two, but this dessert deserves four little custards. If Meyer lemons aren't available, use a combination of orange and lemon zest and juice instead.

1½ cups heavy cream

2 teaspoons grated and finely chopped fresh Meyer lemon zest, plus 1 teaspoon juice

⅜ cup sugar

3 large egg yolks

1 teaspoon vanilla extract

Pinch of salt

Preheat the oven to 325°F.

In a small saucepan, combine the cream and Meyer lemon zest and bring to a simmer over low heat; remove from the stove and let cool for at least 5 minutes.

In a medium bowl, combine the sugar and egg yolks and whisk until the mixture begins to thicken, about 3 to 4 minutes. Gently whisk in the cream mixture. Add the vanilla, lemon juice, and salt. Let the mixture sit for 10 to 15 minutes, then strain through a fine-meshed sieve into four ¾-cup custard cups or ramekins.

Place the ramekins in a baking pan and add enough boiling water to reach halfway up the sides of the ramekins. Bake until firm in the center but still trembling, about 45 to 50 minutes. Remove from the water bath and chill for about 2 to 3 hours in the refrigerator before serving.

Individual Plum, Apricot, and Blueberry Crisps
with Heavy Cream

This American classic can be made with whatever fruit is in season.

Butter for greasing the ramekins

2 black plums, pitted, halved, and quartered

2 apricots, pitted, halved, and quartered

2 cups fresh or frozen blueberries

3 tablespoons sugar

1 tablespoon all-purpose flour

TOPPING

½ cup old-fashioned oats

3 tablespoons all-purpose flour

¼ cup packed dark brown sugar

½ teaspoon ground cinnamon

¼ teaspoon salt

4 tablespoons unsalted butter, melted

Heavy cream (3 to 4 tablespoons per crisp)

Preheat the oven to 400°F. Butter two 1¼-cup ramekins or custard cups.

In a medium bowl, combine the plums, apricots, blueberries, sugar, and flour. Pour the fruit mixture into the prepared ramekins.

FOR THE TOPPING: Combine the oats, flour, dark brown sugar, cinnamon, and salt in a bowl. Mix thoroughly. Add the melted butter and stir until blended. Spread evenly over the top of the fruit in each of the ramekins.

Bake for 25 minutes, or until the topping is brown and the fruit bubbles. Let cool for 5 minutes before serving. Serve with heavy cream.

Fresh Crêpes with Blood Orange, Powdered Sugar, and Candied Blood Orange Rind

These simple crêpes are a wonderful, light finish to a filling meal, or can be a fun afternoon treat with a cup of tea.

1 blood orange

3 tablespoons sugar

1 cup all-purpose flour

3 tablespoons powdered sugar, plus more for garnishing

1 tablespoon unsalted butter, melted

1¼ cups milk

1 large egg

¼ teaspoon vanilla extract

1 teaspoon canola oil

Place a piece of wax paper on the counter next to the stove.

Using a zester or sharp knife, cut the blood orange rind into fifteen ⅛-inch-thick strips, each 1 to 2 inches long. Juice the orange.

In a small saucepan, combine the sugar with ½ cup of water and cook over medium heat for 3 minutes or until syrupy. Add the orange rind to the syrup and cook for 15 to 20 minutes more, or until there is barely any syrup left. Spread the candied orange rind out on the waxed paper to cool.

In a medium bowl, combine the flour and powdered sugar. In another bowl, combine the melted butter, milk, egg, and vanilla. Whisk thoroughly, then add the dry ingredients. Whisk the mixture until smooth.

In a small crêpe pan or sauté pan, heat the canola oil for 2 to 3 minutes, until it is very hot. Remove from the heat and pour about ¼ cup of batter into the pan, swirling the batter around to cover the bottom of the pan. Place the pan back on the stove and cook until golden, about 30 to 45 seconds. Turn the crêpe over and cook for an additional 15 to 20 seconds. Transfer to a plate and repeat.

When you have completed 2 to 4 crêpes, drizzle blood orange juice in the center of each, sprinkle with powdered sugar to taste, then fold them by thirds, first bringing one side inward, then the other. Place the candied orange rind on top, drizzle with more orange juice, and dust with more powdered sugar.

Bananas Flambé with Heavy Cream

When I was a child this was one of my favorite desserts, and it still is. Not only is the gooey, caramelized texture wonderful, but it's also served warm, which gives it that extra comforting feeling. Also, the fact that you ignite the pan makes it magical.

2 tablespoons butter

2 bananas, slightly green, peeled and cut lengthwise

2 tablespoons sugar

2 tablespoons dark rum

2 tablespoons cold heavy cream

Melt the butter in a large sauté pan over medium heat. Lay the bananas in the butter and sprinkle with the sugar, then sauté until browned, about 3 to 4 minutes, turning occasionally.

Heat the rum in a small saucepan until warm. Add the rum to the bananas, then carefully tip the sauté pan over the flame to ignite and burn off the alcohol. If using an electric stove, use a flame ignitor or a match (but an ignitor is less dangerous) to ignite the rum.

Divide the bananas into two bowls, drizzle with the caramelized rum butter, then drizzle with the cold heavy cream and serve.

Poached Vanilla Pears
with Fresh Vanilla Ice Cream

Tender and delicate, these pears make a subtle, sublime dessert with the fresh ice cream.

2 tablespoons unsalted butter

½ cup sugar

Grated and finely chopped zest of 2 fresh lemons

1½ cups dry white wine

1 whole vanilla bean

2 medium-ripe Barlett or Bosc pears, peeled, cored, and quartered

Fresh Vanilla Ice Cream (page 102)

In a medium-large saucepan, combine the butter, sugar, lemon zest, and white wine. Slice the vanilla bean in half lengthwise and scrape the seeds from the pod into the liquid. Cook the liquid over medium heat for 4 minutes until it thickens into a syrup.

Add the pears to the liquid and cook for 20 to 25 minutes, or until tender to the touch. Spoon the syrup over the pears several times as they cook. Serve warm with the Fresh Vanilla Ice Cream.

Fresh Vanilla Ice Cream

| 1 ½ cups milk | ¾ cup sugar | 2 large egg yolks |
| 1 whole vanilla bean | ¼ teaspoon salt | 2 cups heavy cream |

In a medium saucepan, heat the milk over low heat until bubbles form around the edges of the pan. Split the vanilla bean in half lengthwise, scrape the seeds into the milk, then add the pod. Cook, while stirring, for 1 to 2 minutes. Stir in the sugar and salt until dissolved. Remove from the heat and let cool for 10 minutes. Remove the vanilla pod.

In a small stainless-steel bowl, beat the egg yolks. Slowly add the milk mixture to the eggs. Whisk until combined. Set the bowl over a saucepan of barely simmering water. Cook, stirring constantly, for 10 to 12 minutes or until the mixture is thick enough to coat the back of the spoon. Remove from the heat and let cool.

Cover and refrigerate for at least 1 hour. Stir in the cream. Refrigerate for 1 more hour. Freeze in an ice cream maker according to the manufacturer's instructions.

Broiled Fresh Figs and Sweet Gorgonzola, Drizzled with Honey

I can't think of a fruit I love more than figs. In late summer when Mission figs are in season, I walk through my neighborhood and pluck ripe, juicy ones from friendly neighbors' trees. (I'm known in my Los Angeles canyon as "the congenial figoholic.") Though they're divine just plain, here's an elegant, sumptuous way to serve them for dessert.

5 ripe black Mission figs

2 tablespoons sweet Gorgonzola, crumbled

1 tablespoon honey

2 sprigs fresh mint for garnish

Preheat the oven to broil.

Slice the figs in half lengthwise and place them cut side down on a 4-by-4-inch glass baking dish. Place under the broiler for 3 to 4 minutes, or until they begin to caramelize. Scatter the sweet Gorgonzola pieces around the figs, and return to the broiler for 1 to 2 minutes more or until the cheese begins to become runny.

Transfer the caramelized figs and runny Gorgonzola onto 2 small decorative plates. Drizzle with the honey, top with a sprig of mint, and serve.

Individual Croissant Bread Puddings
with **Dried Cherries, Bittersweet Chocolate,** and **Toasted Pecans**

This is probably my favorite dessert in the book. It looks and tastes like you struggled all day, yet from start to finish it takes less than 45 minutes to prepare (and 25 minutes of that is baking).

¼ cup dried cherries

¼ cup pecans

Canola oil for greasing

2 cups heavy cream

1 vanilla bean

4 large egg yolks

1½ cups sugar

¼ teaspoon salt

3 day-old croissants

2 tablespoons coarsely grated bittersweet chocolate (from about 1 ounce)

Preheat the oven to broil.

Put the cherries in a small bowl, cover with boiling water, and let sit for 20 minutes, then drain.

Spread the pecans out in a pie tin, place on the middle rack of the oven, and carefully watch for 1 to 2 minutes or until the nuts are golden. Cool, then chop.

Preheat the oven to 350°F. Grease two ovenproof bowls (with 4-inch diameters) with canola oil.

Add the heavy cream to a medium saucepan. Slice the vanilla bean in half lengthwise and scrape the seeds from the pod into the liquid, then add the pod. Simmer over low heat for 8 to 10 minutes, then remove the vanilla bean pod.

Combine the egg yolks, sugar, and salt in a medium bowl and whisk together. Slowly pour in the cream mixture while whisking.

Tear the croissants into 6 pieces each and place in a medium bowl, then cover with the cream and egg mixture. Allow the croissants to absorb the liquid for about 10 minutes. Add the cherries.

Transfer the mixture to the prepared bowls and sprinkle the top of each bowl with the chocolate and toasted pecans. Place the puddings in the oven and bake for 25 minutes or until set, then serve.

Phyllo Nests Filled with Raspberries and Drizzled with Orange Syrup and Bittersweet Chocolate

I love using phyllo dough in desserts. The light, crisp dough goes beautifully with almost any filling, plus it's so simple to prepare. In the past, I've made a more traditional, Greek-inspired version of phyllo nests with walnuts and honey, but this one is much more interesting. This recipe makes four phyllo nests. I figure if you bought the phyllo you might as well make four nests; they can be kept for up to three days in an airtight container.

6 tablespoons sugar

2 teaspoons freshly grated and finely chopped orange zest

4 sheets thawed frozen phyllo dough

4 tablespoons melted butter

2 ounces high-quality bittersweet chocolate

1 cup fresh raspberries

Preheat the oven to 425°F.

In a small saucepan, combine the sugar, ½ cup water, and the orange zest, and cook until syrupy, about 7 to 8 minutes. Set aside.

Working with one sheet of phyllo at a time, pick a sheet up from the center (as you would a handkerchief) and begin twisting the phyllo as you set it down again on a baking sheet to make a free-form "nest" 3 to 4 inches in diameter. Using a pastry brush, brush the nest liberally with the melted butter. Then brush with the orange syrup. Repeat for each nest.

Bake the phyllo for 15 minutes, or until crisp and golden. Remove from the oven and let cool.

In a double boiler, melt the chocolate until smooth and runny, then remove from the heat.

To serve the dessert, place each nest in the center of a plate. Liberally drizzle with the remaining warm orange syrup, then the warm bittersweet chocolate, and sprinkle with the raspberries.

INDEX

P

Table of Equivalents

The exact equivalents in the following tables have been rounded for convenience.

Liquid/Dry Measurements

U.S.	Metric
¼ teaspoon	1.25 milliliters
½ teaspoon	2.5 milliliters
1 teaspoon	5 milliliters
1 tablespoon (3 teaspoons)	15 milliliters
1 fluid ounce (2 tablespoons)	30 milliliters
¼ cup	60 milliliters
⅓ cup	80 milliliters
½ cup	120 milliliters
1 cup	240 milliliters
1 pint (2 cups)	480 milliliters
1 quart (4 cups, 32 ounces)	960 milliliters
1 gallon (4 quarts)	3.84 liters
1 ounce (by weight)	28 grams
1 pound	448 grams
2.2 pounds	1 kilogram

Lengths

U.S.	Metric
⅛ inch	3 millimeters
¼ inch	6 millimeters
½ inch	12 millimeters
1 inch	2.5 centimeters

Oven Temperature

Fahrenheit	Celsius	Gas
250	120	½
275	140	1
300	150	2
325	160	3
350	180	4
375	190	5
400	200	6
425	220	7
450	230	8
475	240	9
500	260	10